Preface

Dedicated to my son, Ali, who has taught me the meaning of love. This story is a gift from me on his 6th birthday to remind him of the greatness he is capable of and to learn the 'Art of Giving' that his grandparents have passed on.

Tabassum Nafsi

Once upon a time, in a land far away, there lived a young boy named Ali. He lived there with his parents, his younger sisters, Aria, and baby Zarah.

It was the month of December. The spirit of the holiday season had filled the air with joy, peace, and love.

Ali's birthday was coming up soon too. He was excited. Every morning, he would wake up and ask "Alexa" how many more days until his birthday.

One fine morning, Ali woke up and saw snow in the front yard. Trees, bushes and the fields were covered with snow. It was beautiful. He got out of bed, cleaned up his room and said: "Alexa! How many days until December 18th?"

Alexa replied: "December 18th is in one day."

Ali jumped with excitement and ran down the stairs. He saw his mother in the kitchen preparing breakfast and getting ready to leave for work. "It's my birthday tomorrow," said Ali.

Mom replied, "Yes, it's a big day. You turn 6 tomorrow!"

The next morning, Ali woke up and found his room filled with balloons and a card from his mom. The card said:

"Today I gift you 'The Art of Giving.'

With love and hope,

Mom."

'The Art of Giving.' "Hmm! I wonder what that means", thought Ali. After breakfast, his mom asked him to get ready so that they could go out for a mother-son birthday lunch.

They stopped at their favorite burger place and then grabbed an ice cream. After that, they stopped at the bank.

His mother greeted the teller and said, "This is my son, Ali. He turned 6 today. I would like to open a bank account for him." "Certainly, madam," said the teller. She filled in the details for the family account and handed over a bank ATM card to Ali.

"Here you are," said his mom, "From today you have your own bank account. You, my dear, will manage your account and every year on your birthday, I will ask you to give me something."

"What can I give you, Mama?" asked Ali. "I don't want it for myself," she replied. "I want you to give 20% of your annual savings to someone in need or a charity. Just learn to give. Can you do that?"

"20%! What is that?" asked Ali. "20% means 1/5th. For example, if you have $5 saved at the end of the year, then you give $1 away. Do you think you can manage that?" asked his mother.

"Oh ok! I can do that, easily!" said Ali.

For the first few years, his mother helped him calculate the amount to be given away. Later, each year on his birthday, Ali would calculate 20% of his savings and would write a check to a charity organization called, "Khamsa."

Years passed and Ali did that annually without even thinking twice. Each time, he would write a hand-written card that said: "The Art of Giving. Pass it on!"

Ali was now 18 and had joined college. For the last few years, he had started saving a lot more for his college tuition. This year, after paying his fees, he wasn't left with a lot.

On his birthday, he decided to forgo his annual savings check to "Khamsa." "I am older now," he thought to himself, "What good does this little amount of money do in this world anyway?" "I need to save more for myself."

On his first day at his college, Ali had met a boy called, "Yusuf." They quickly became good friends.

One day after college, Ali stopped at Yusuf's house to pick him up for a soccer game that evening. On his way, Yusuf requested Ali to stop at an ATM machine. "I need to withdraw some cash," said Yusuf.

Once there, Yusuf withdrew $200 and put it in an envelope. He wrote: "The Art of Giving. Pass it on!" on it. This act caught Ali by surprise.

Next, Yusuf asked Ali to drive him to a neighborhood across the bridge. There were small homes in this area with run down streets. Yusuf asked Ali to stop outside a house and left the envelope in the mailbox. "Turn around and drive away quietly, please", Yusuf whispered.

Ali was puzzled and asked Yusuf, "Whose house is that and why did you leave money in their mailbox?"

Yusuf said, "This goes back many years," as he pulled out his wallet from his front pocket. He showed Ali a handwritten card that said: 'The Art of Giving. Pass it on!'

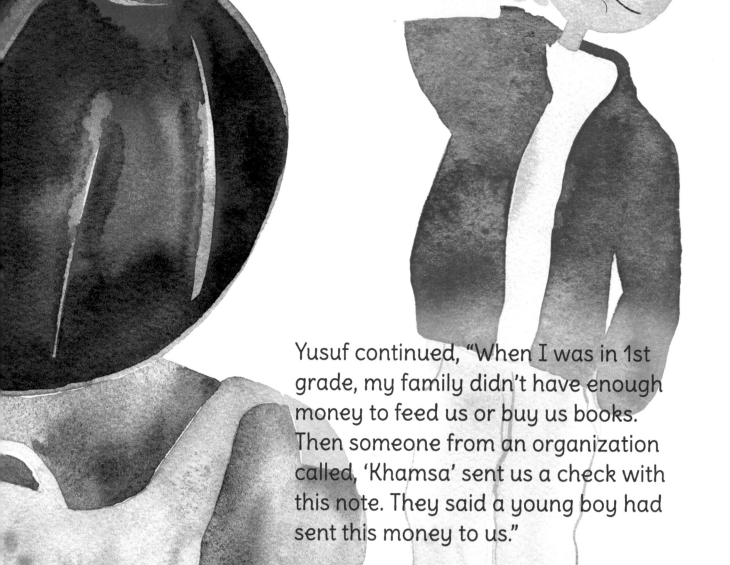

Yusuf continued, "When I was in 1st grade, my family didn't have enough money to feed us or buy us books. Then someone from an organization called, 'Khamsa' sent us a check with this note. They said a young boy had sent this money to us."

Ali took a closer look at that note. It was the same note he had written on his 6th birthday when he had mailed his first check.

"We used to get that check every year and it helped pay for my tuition. When my father got a job, the checks stopped coming as we did not need them anymore. Today I am in college because of this kid who I don't even know," said Yusuf, with a humble note in his voice.

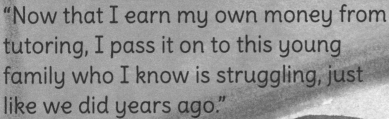

"Now that I earn my own money from tutoring, I pass it on to this young family who I know is struggling, just like we did years ago."

Ali's eyes filled with tears. He hugged Yusuf and told him how generous he was. "I will do the same," he said as he realizes what a big mistake he was about to make.

Ali drove to the soccer game
with Yusuf, deep in thought.
His mother arrived at the
field too straight from work.

Ali ran to her and hugged her tightly and
whispered in her ear, "Now I know what you
gave me on my 6th birthday. It was the best
gift ever and I didn't even realize it then." Ali's
mother returned his hug as she sensed that the
seed she had wanted to plant in Ali's heart many
years ago, had finally taken root.

"I will continue this gift of giving and hope that others pass it on as well. Kindness goes a long way, indeed," he said to his mother. "Yes, it does," she said as she recalls the moment with her mother, when she too, had learned that lesson.

Ali

CPSIA information can be obtained
at www.ICGtesting.com
Printed in the USA
BVHW021221220321
603176BV00003B/14